Warming Up for Bass

book one

by Cassia Harvey

Edited by Matthew Roberts

CHP121
ISBN 978-1-932823-20-2

6403 N. 6th Street
Philadelphia, PA 19126
www.charveypublications.com

Less-advanced (A) pages are structured so that they can be played together with more-advanced (B) pages.

Contents

Warmups in G major

Daily Exercise (A)

Cassia Harvey

Edited by Matthew Roberts

March (A)

L. Mozart, arr. Harvey

3

Daily Exercise (B)

Warming Up for Bass, Book One

March (B)

L. Mozart, arr. Harvey

Warming Up for Bass, Book One

Finger Workout (A)

Sonata (A)

Cimarosa, arr. Harvey

8

Finger Workout (B)

Sonata (B)

Cimarosa, arr. Harvey

Finger Twister (A)

Warming Up for Bass, Book One

Dill Pickle Rag (A)

Johnson, arr. Harvey

Warming Up for Bass, Book One

Finger Twister (B)

Warming Up for Bass, Book One

Dill Pickle Rag (B)

Johnson, arr. Harvey

Warmups in D major

Daily Exercise (A)

Variations on a Theme (A)

Romberg, arr. Harvey

Daily Exercise (B)

Variations on a Theme (B)

Romberg, arr. Harvey

Finger Workout (A)

Rondo (A)

Mozart, arr. Harvey

Finger Workout (B)

Rondo (B)

Mozart, arr. Harvey

Finger Twister (A)

Miss Ratray's Reel (A)

Trad., arr. Harvey

Finger Twister (B)

Miss Ratray's Reel (B)

Trad., arr. Harvey

Warmups in C major

Daily Exercise (A)

Mason's Apron (A)

Trad., arr. Harvey

Daily Exercise (B)

Mason's Apron (B)

Trad., arr. Harvey

Warming Up for Bass, Book One

Finger Workout (A)

Bourree (A)

Bach, arr. Harvey

Finger Workout (B)

Bourree (B)

Bach, arr. Harvey

Finger Twister (A)

Grazioso (A)

Cimarosa, arr. Harvey

35

Finger Twister (B)

Grazioso (B)

Cimarosa, arr. Harvey

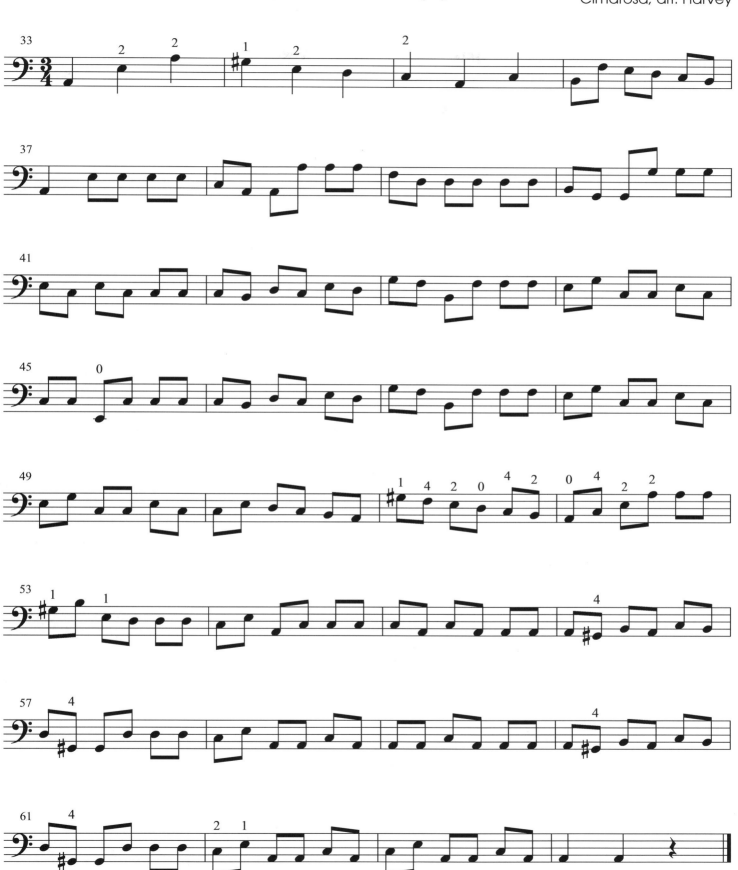

Warmups in F major

Daily Exercise (A)

Variation (A)

Paganini, arr. Harvey

Warming Up for Bass, Book One

Daily Exercise (B)

Variation (B)

Paganini, arr. Harvey

Finger Workout (A)

Allegro (A)

Paxton, arr. Harvey

43

Finger Workout (B)

Allegro (B)

Paxton, arr. Harvey

Warming Up for Bass, Book One

Finger Twister (A)

The Dashing Sergeant (A)

Trad., arr. Harvey

Finger Twister (B)

Warming Up for Bass, Book One

The Dashing Sergeant (B)

Trad., arr. Harvey

Warming Up for Bass, Book One

Made in the USA
Las Vegas, NV
06 August 2023